Baby Sign Language

Official Reference Dictionary

Table of Contents

Introduction

The Baby Sign Language Dictionary includes more than 600 of the most commonly used signs in Baby Sign Language. We suggest using this book in conjunction with our online video dictionary (www.BabySignLanguage.com/dictionary), particularly when learning a sign for the first time. We find that the online videos better convey the signing motion, while the diagrams better convey finger positioning.

The signs used in this book are American Sign Language (ASL), which is the predominant sign language in the United States. Certain signs in this dictionary may be depicted differently in other books or by other ASL users. This is due to the existence of several acceptable variations for many words in ASL. For signs with variations, we provide the simplest variation.

Should you need a word not found in this dictionary, consult a comprehensive ASL dictionary (e.g., www.ASLpro.com or www.lifeprint.com).

Left and Right Handed Signing

The illustrations in the dictionary are based on right handed signing. When signing, your dominant hand plays the starring role and your non-dominant hand plays the supporting role. If you are right handed, the action part of the sign will be formed with your right hand. If you are left handed, the left hand will do most of the action and the right hand will play the supporting role.

You may reverse hands if it is more convenient. For example, if you are right handed and holding your baby with your right hand, feel free to sign with your left hand.

Conventions

Two or more diagrams are provided for each sign. The first (left-most) diagram shows the starting position for your hands and indicates the direction of motion. The final diagram shows the ending position for your hands. Let's use *cat* as an example.

Cat

Starting Position and Motion	**Ending Position**

To sign *cat*, start with your dominant hand by the side of your face, with your thumb and index finger extended (left diagram). From that starting point, bring your thumb and index finger together, then move your hand away from your face (right diagram). The *cat* sign resembles a person pulling on a whisker.

Comments are welcome. E-mail us at dictionary@babysignlanguage.com, connect with us through our website at www.BabySignLanguage.com, or join our Facebook community at www.facebook.com/babysignlang.

Aa

A

Airplane

All Done

All Gone

Alligator

Ambulance

Angry

Animal

Apple

Art

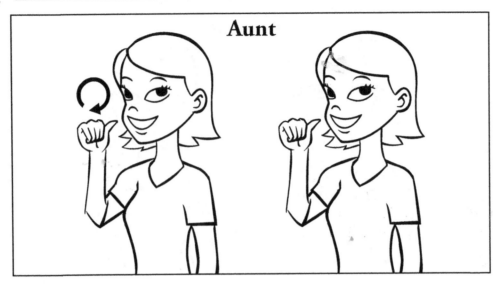

Aunt

Bb

B

Baby

Babysitter

Backpack

Bacon

Bad

Bag

Ball

Balloon

Banana

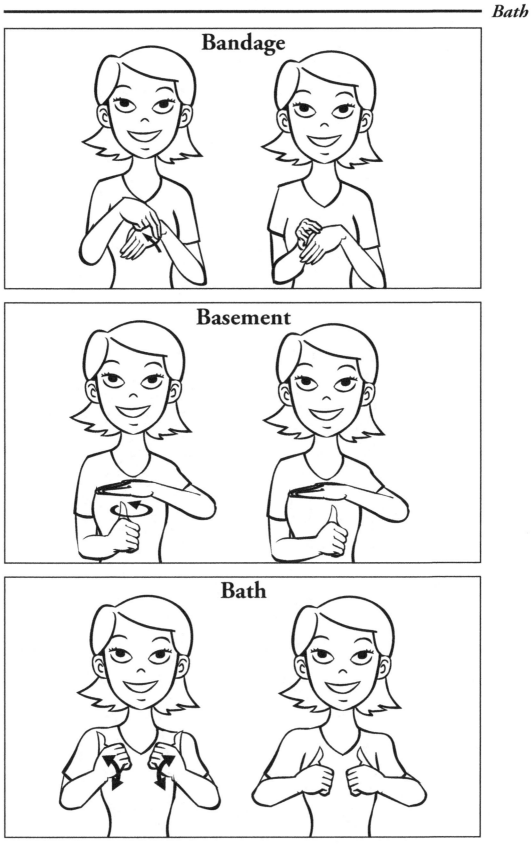

Bandage

Basement

Bath

Battery

Be Careful

Beach

Bean

Bear

Beautiful

Bed

Bedroom

Bee

Behave

Bell

Belt

Bib

Bicycle

Big

Bird

Birthday

Black

Blanket

Blocks

Blonde

Blue

Boat

Book

Boots

Bottle

Bowl

Box

Boy

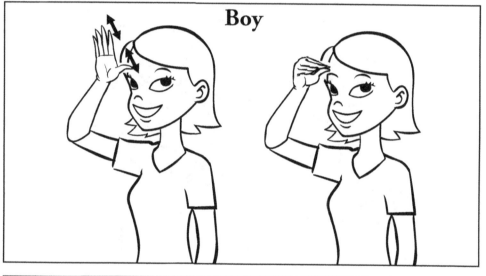

Bracelet

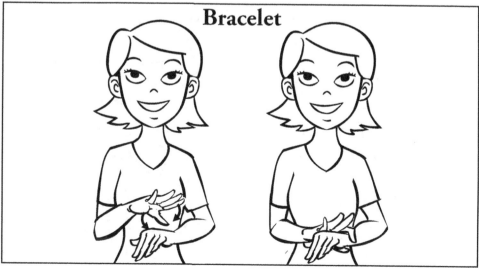

Bread

Breakfast

Breast Feed

Breast Milk

Broken

Brother

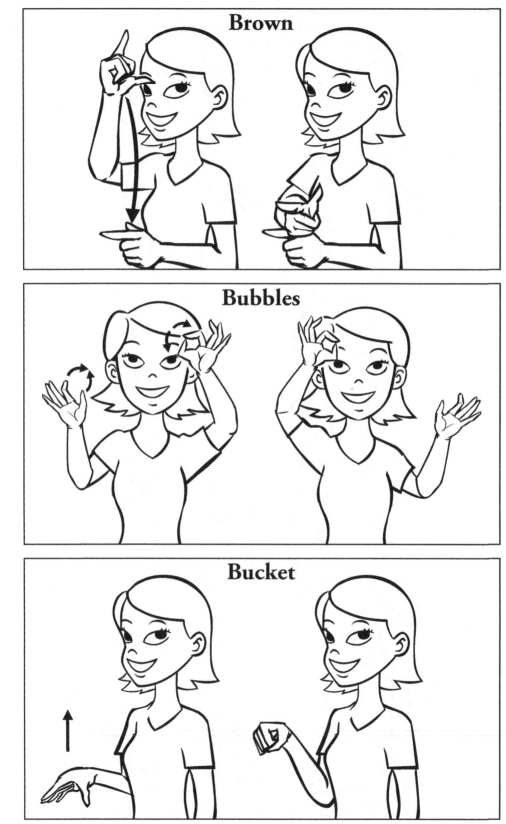

Brown

Bubbles

Bucket

Bug

Build

Bunny

Bus

Busy

Butter

Butterfly

Button

Bye Bye

Cc

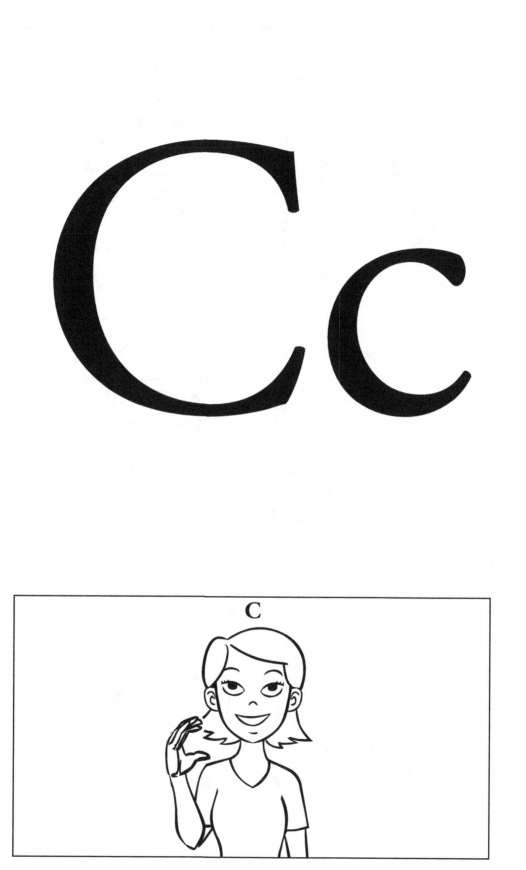

C

Cage

Cake

Camera

Candle

Candy

Car

Cards

Cat

Caterpillar

Cereal

Chair

Change

Cheese

Cherry

Chicken

Children

Chocolate

Christmas

Church

Circle

Class

Clothes

Cloud

Clown

Coat

Cold

Color

Come

Computer

Cook

Cookie

Corn

Count

Cousin

Cow

Crab

Cracker

Crawl

Cry

Cup

Cut

Cute

Dd

D

Daddy

Dance

Dark

Day

Deer

Dentist

Dessert

Diaper

Dining Room

Dinner

Dinosaur

Dirt / Dirty

Doctor

Dog

Doll

Dolphin

Don't

Don't Hit

Door

Door Bell

Down

Dress (garment)

Dress (get dressed)

Drink

Drum

Dry

Duck

E

Ear

Earphone

Earring

Easter

Egg

Elephant

Excited

Excuse Me

Eye Glasses

Ff

F

Fall Down

Family

Fan

Farm

Farmer

Fast

Fat

Favorite

Feel

Fire

Fire Fighter

Fireworks

continued overleaf

Fireworks (continued)

Fish

Fix

Flag

Flashlight

Floor

Flower

Fork

Fox

French Fries

Friend

Frog

Fruit

Frustrated

Full

Fun

Funny

G g

G

Game

Garage

Garbage

Garden

Gate

Gentle

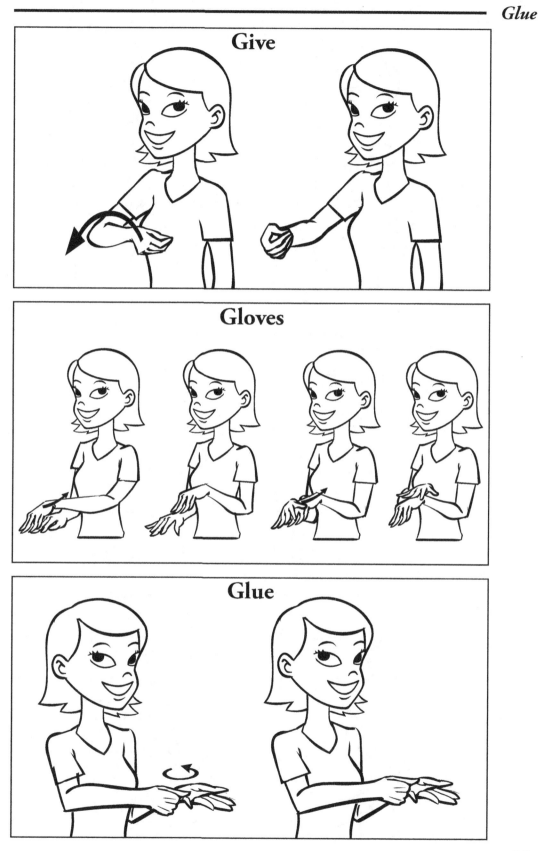

Give

Gloves

Glue

Go

Goat

Good

Good Morning

Good Night

Goose

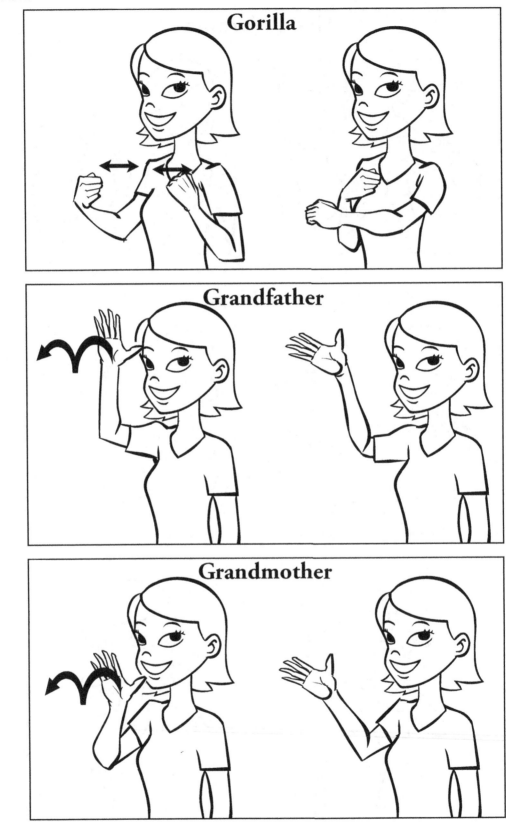

Gorilla

Grandfather

Grandmother

Grapes

Grass

Gray

Green

Grumpy

Guitar

H

Hair

Hair Brush (brush hair)

Hall

Hamburger

Hanukkah

Happy

Hat

Hear

Heart

Helicopter

Hello

Help

High

Hill

Hippopotamus

Hit

Holiday

Horse

Hot

Hotdog

House

How

Hungry

Hurry

Hurt

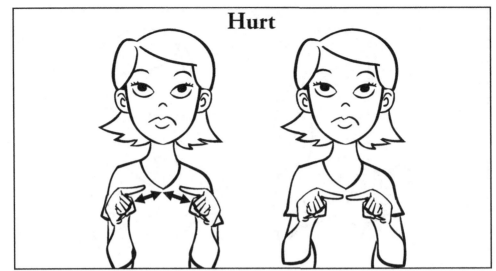

Ii

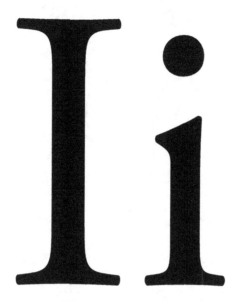

I

I Love You

Ice

Ice Cream

In

Inside

Island

Itch

Jj

J

Jelly (jam)

Juice

Jump

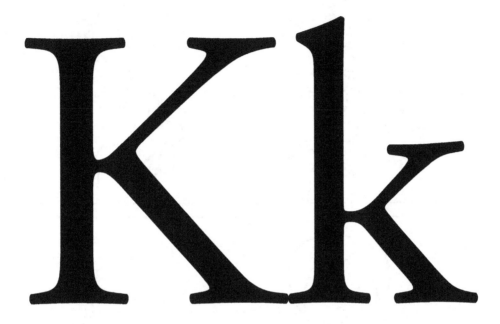

K

Kangaroo

Key

Kick

King

Kiss

Kitchen

Kite

Knife

Ll

L

Ladder

Lake

Lamb

Later

Laugh

Laundry

Leaf

Lemon

Lettuce

Library

Light

Like

Lion

Little

Look At

Love

Lunch

Mm

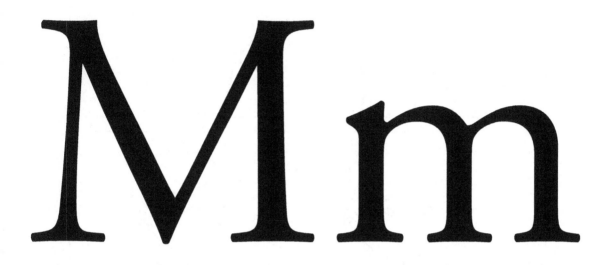

M

Mad

Magazine

Magic

Make

Man

Many

Mask

Meat

Medicine

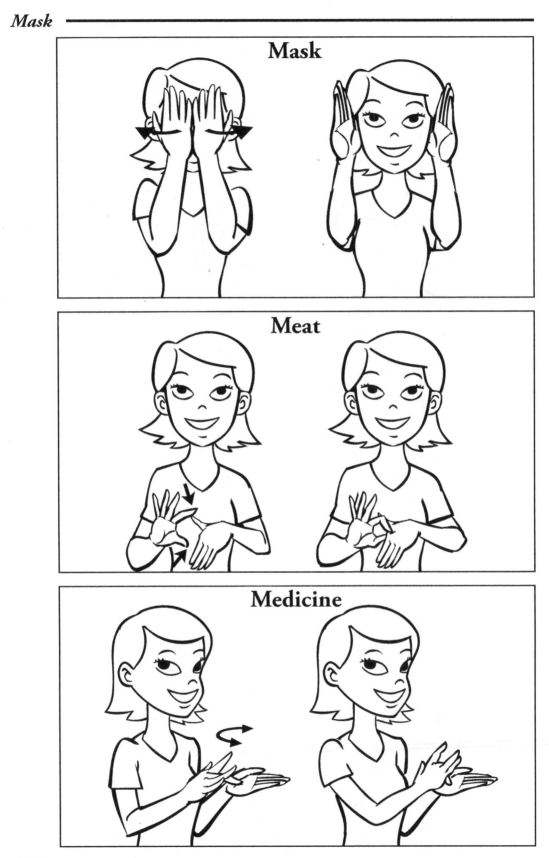

Melon

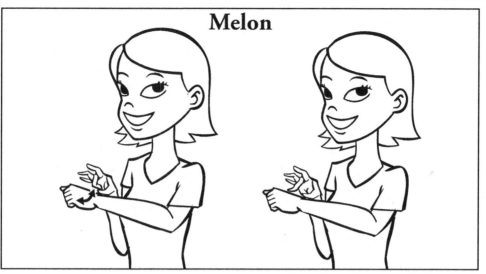

Messy

Microwave

Money

Monkey

Monster

Moon

Moose

More

Motorcycle

Mouse

Movie

Mushroom

Music

N

Naked

Nanny

Napkin

Near

Necklace

Necktie

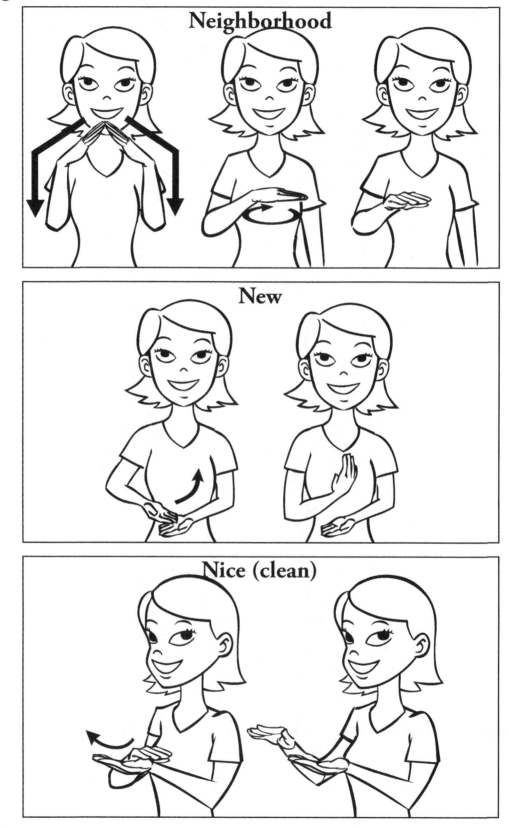

Neighborhood

New

Nice (clean)

Night

Nightmare

No

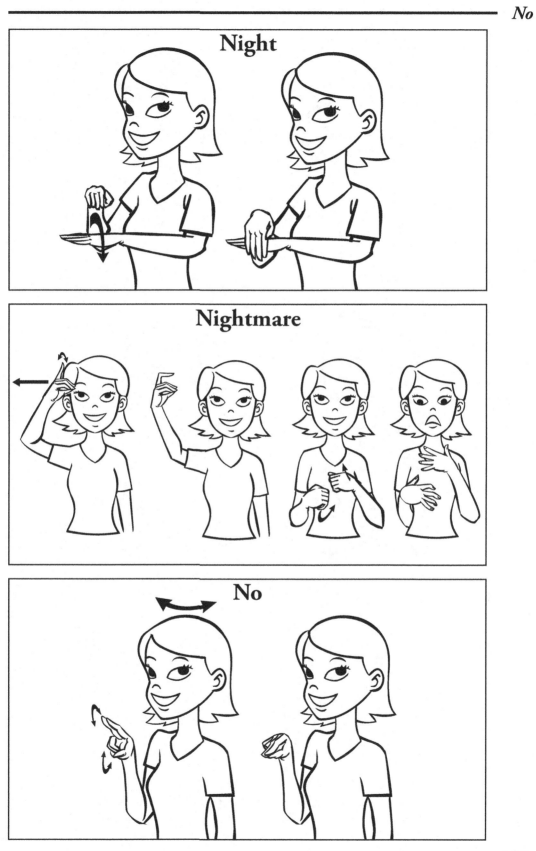

Noise

None

Now

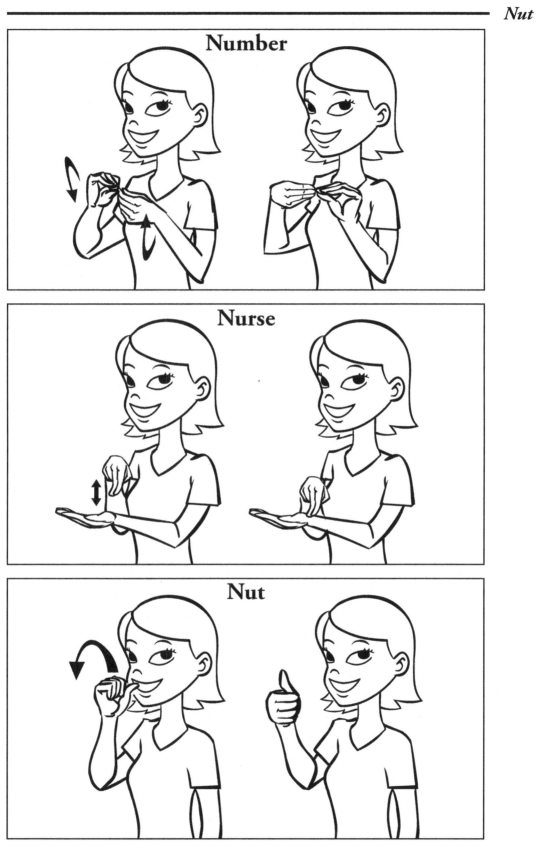

Number

Nurse

Nut

o

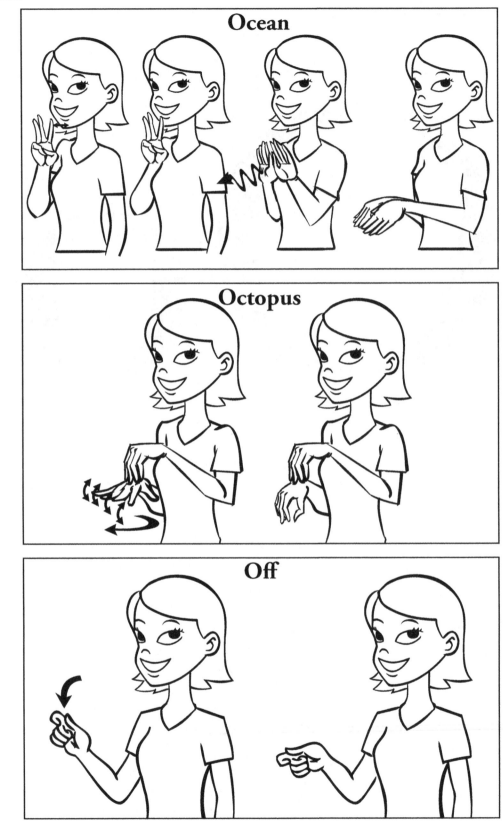

Ocean

Octopus

Off

Old

On

Onion

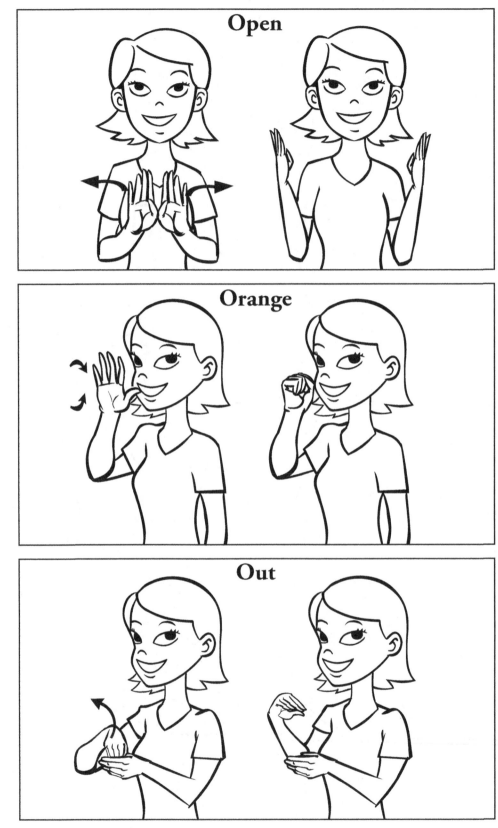

Open

Orange

Out

Outside

Oven

Owl

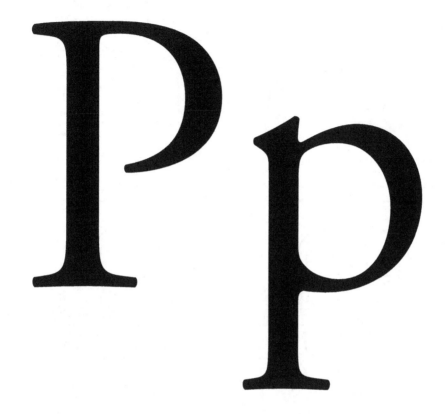

P

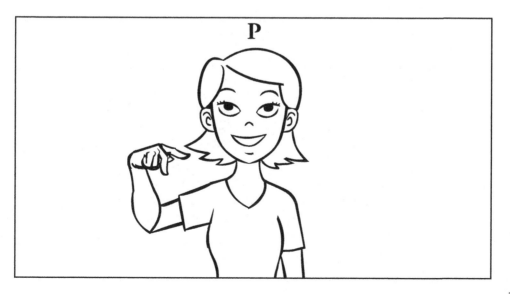

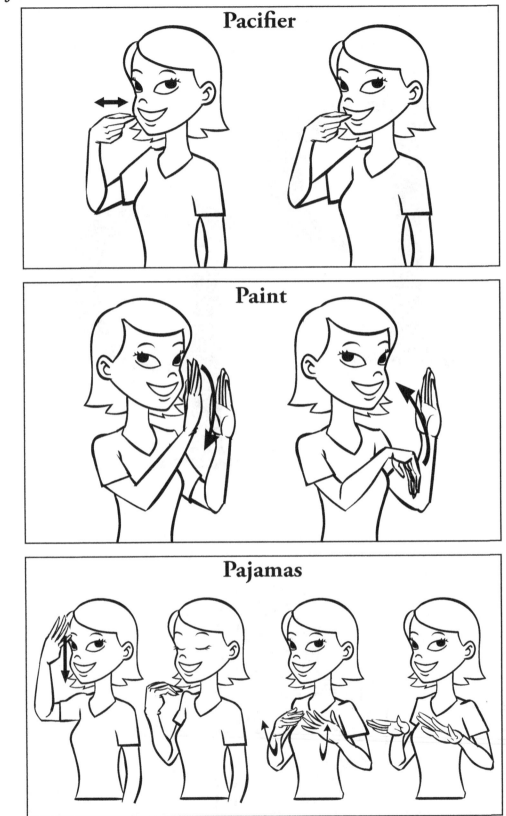

Pacifier

Paint

Pajamas

Pancake

Panda

Pants

Paper

Park

Party

Pasta

Peach

Peanut Butter

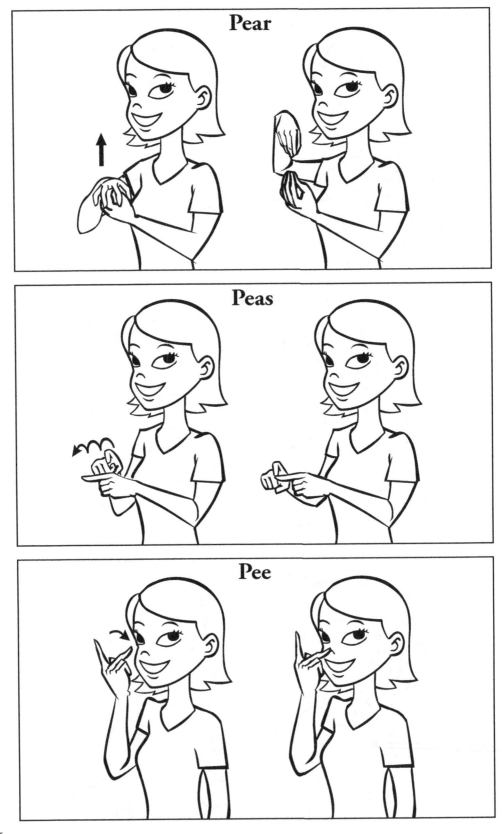

Pear

Peas

Pee

Pen

Phone

Piano

Pickle

Picnic

Pig

Pillow

Pineapple

Pink

Pizza

Plant

Plate

Playground

Please

Plug

Plug

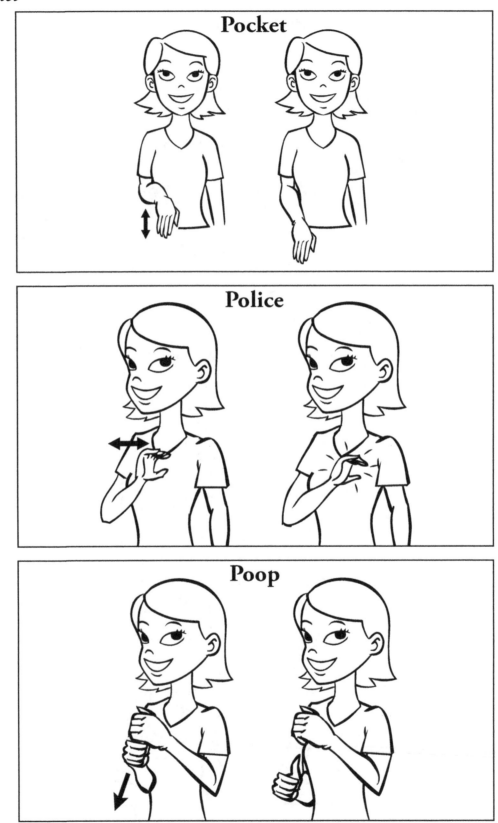

Pocket

Police

Poop

Popcorn

Pot

Potato

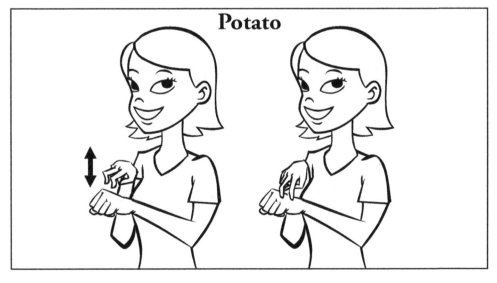

Potty

President

Prince

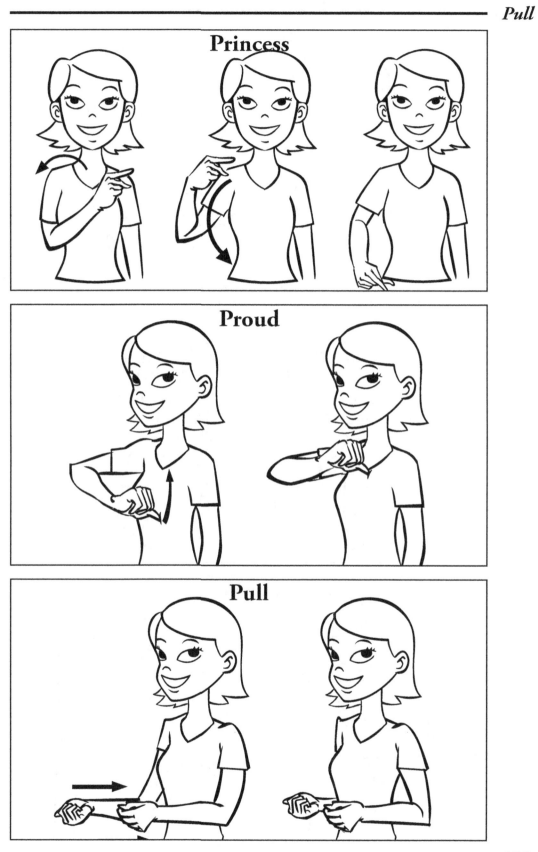

Princess

Proud

Pull

Pumpkin

Puppet

Purple

Push

Put On

Puzzle

Queen

Quiet

Rr

R

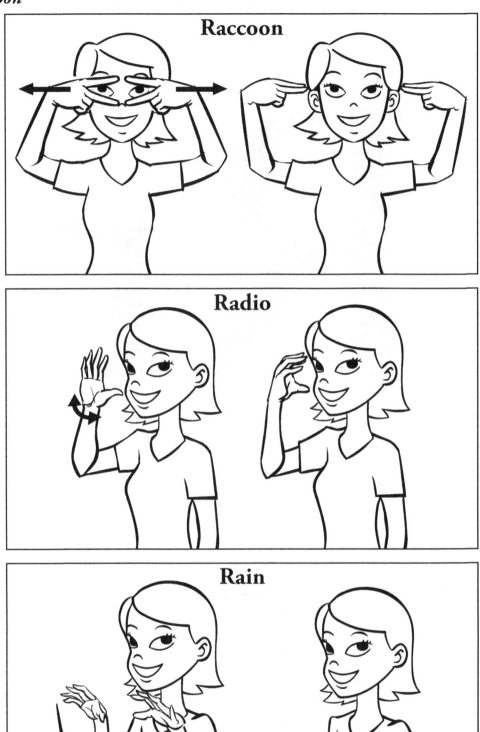

Raccoon

Radio

Rain

Rainbow

Rat

Rattle

Read

Ready

Rectangle

Red

Refrigerator

Reptile

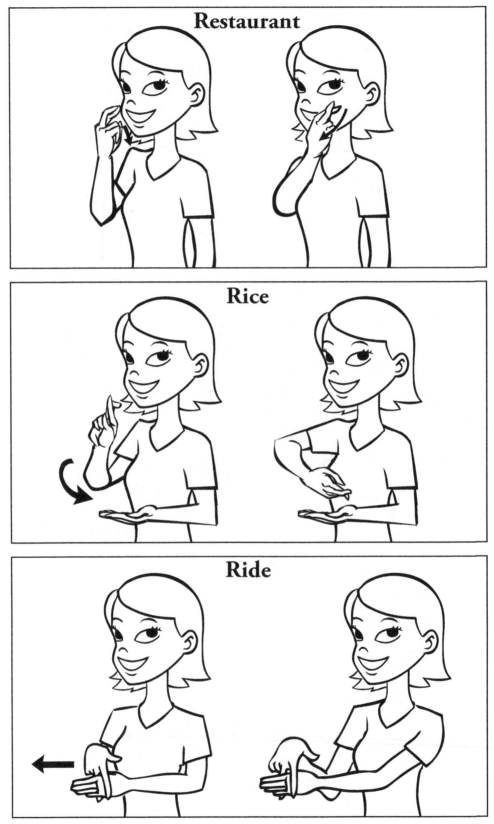

Restaurant

Rice

Ride

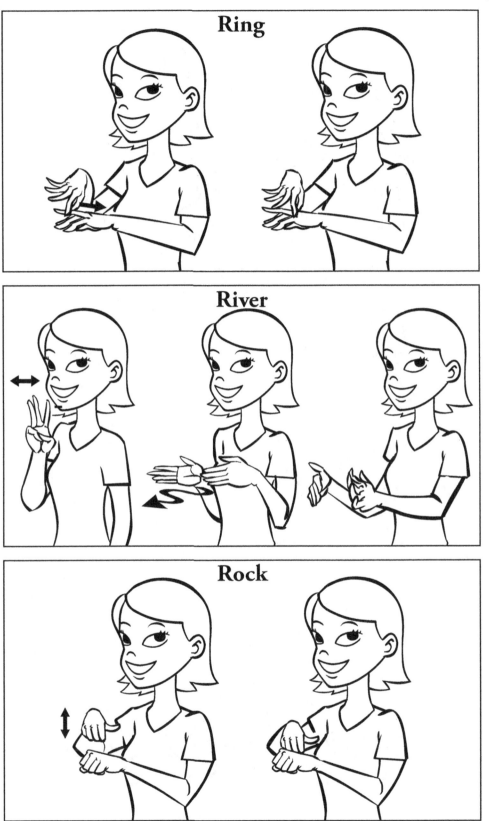

Ring

River

Rock

Roof

Rope

Run

Ss

Sad

Salad

Salt

Same

Sandwich

School

Scissors

Seal

See

Shampoo

Share

Shark

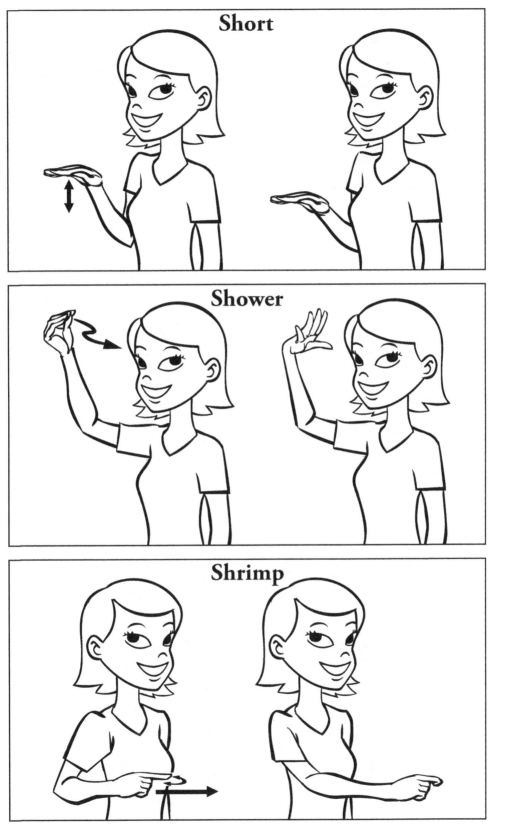

Short

Shower

Shrimp

Shy

Sick

Sign (Sign Language)

Sing

Sink

Sister

Sit

Skate (ice skate)

Skate (roller skate)

Ski

Skunk

Sky

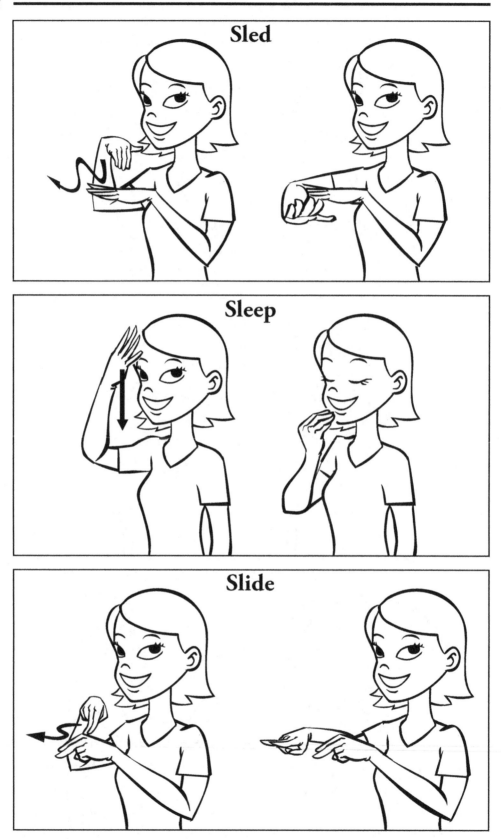

Sled

Sleep

Slide

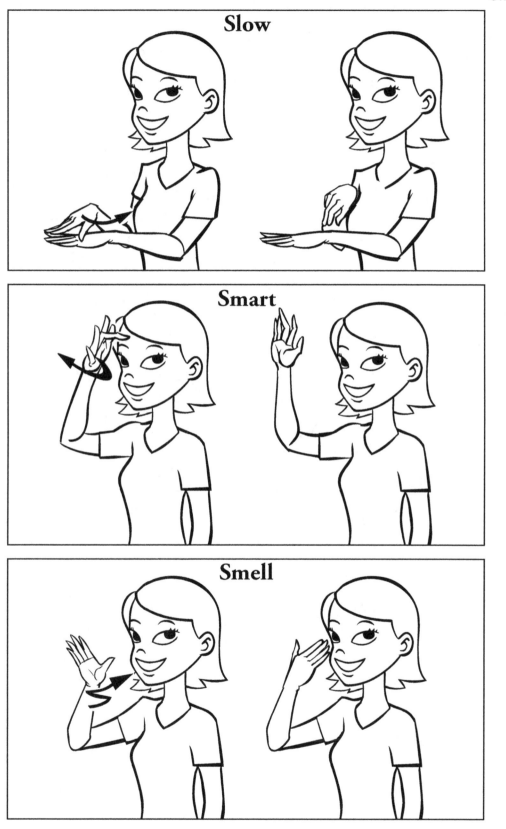

Slow

Smart

Smell

Smile

Snack

Snake

Sneeze

Snow

Soap

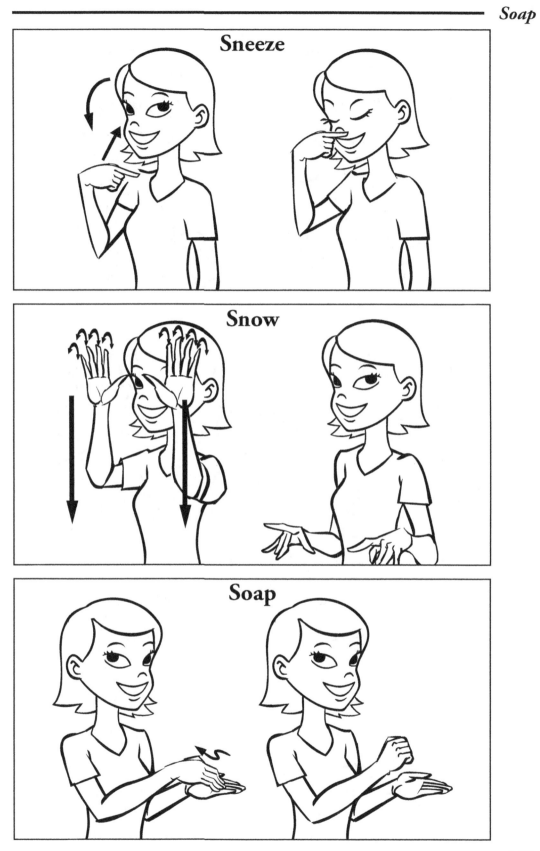

Socks

Sofa

Sorry

Soup

Sour

Spell

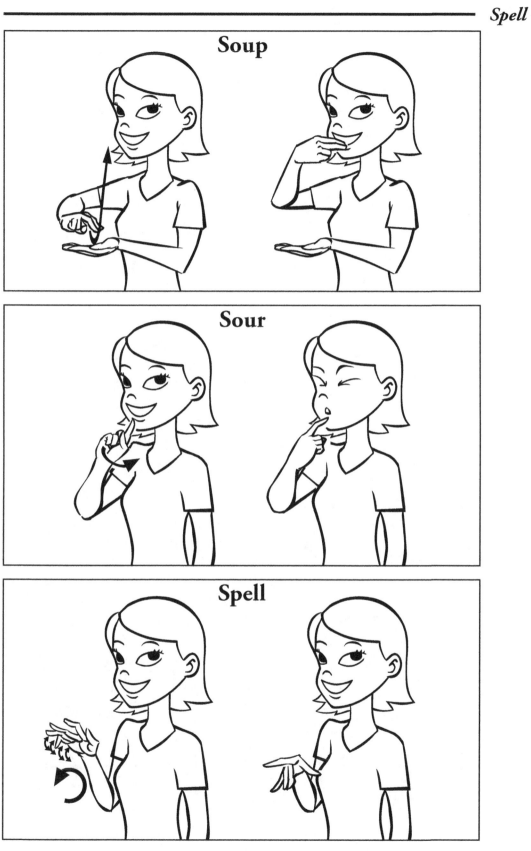

Spider

Spill

Sponge

Spoon

Square

Squirrel

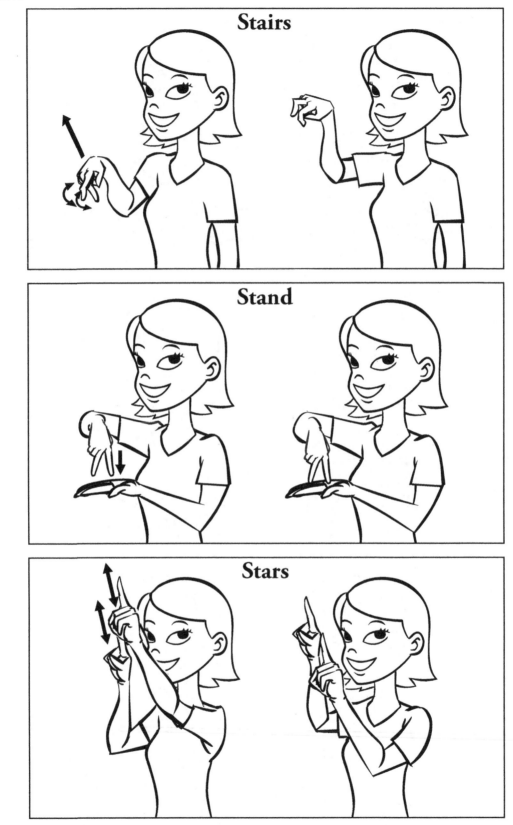

Stairs

Stand

Stars

Start

Stick

Sticky

Stinky

Stop

Store

Strawberry

Street

Stroller

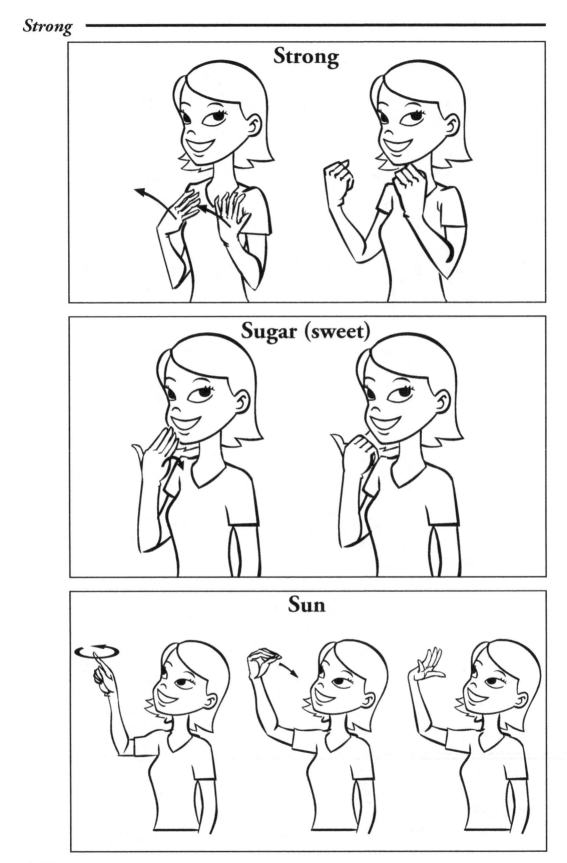

Strong

Sugar (sweet)

Sun

Supermarket

Surprise

Sweater

Sweep

Swim

Swing

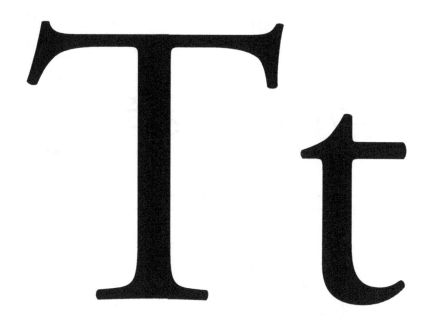

Table

Talk

Tall

Taste

Taxi

Teacher

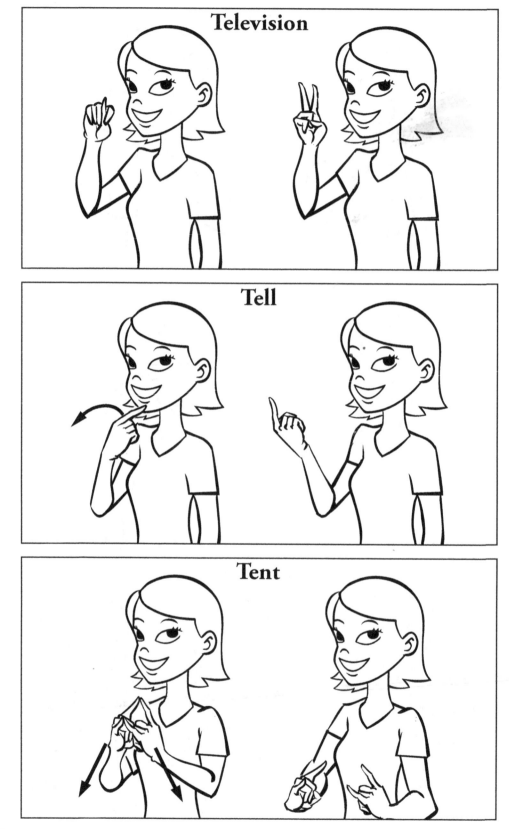

Television

Tell

Tent

Thank You

Thanksgiving

Thick

Thin

Thirsty

Throw Away

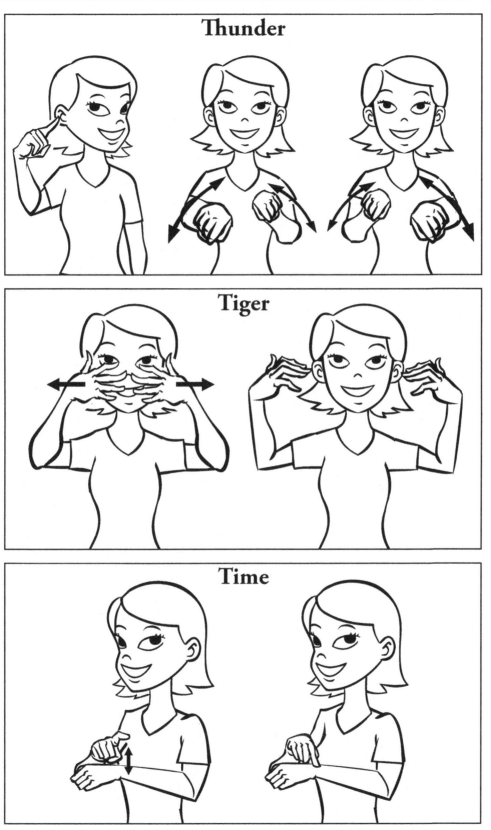

Thunder

Tiger

Time

Tired

Tissue

Toast

Together

Toilet (potty)

Tomato

Toothbrush (brush teeth)

Toothpaste

Touch

Towel

Toy

Train

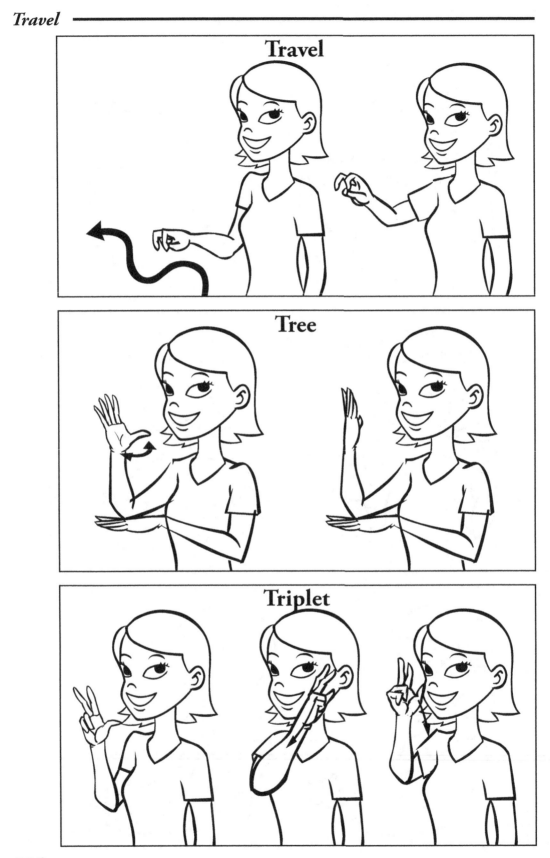

Travel

Tree

Triplet

Truck

Try

Turkey

(my) Turn

(your) Turn

(alternate) Turns

Turtle

Twin

Uu

U

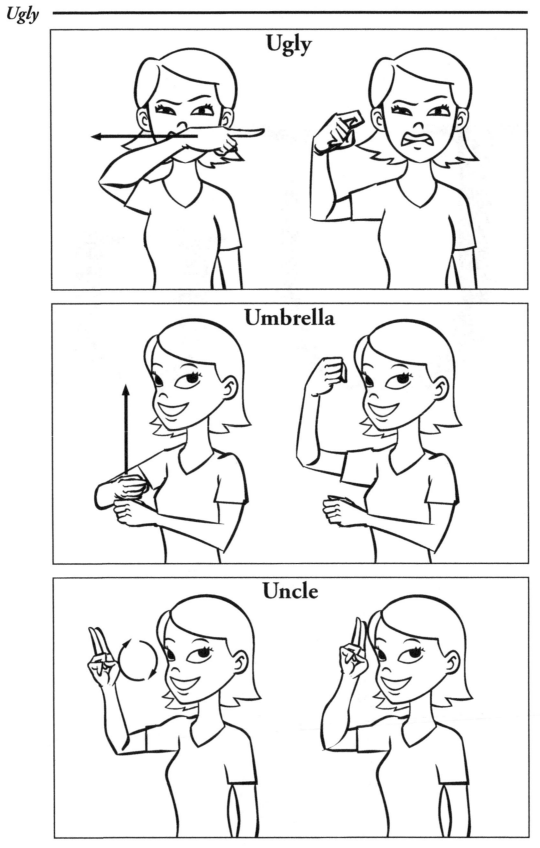

Ugly

Umbrella

Uncle

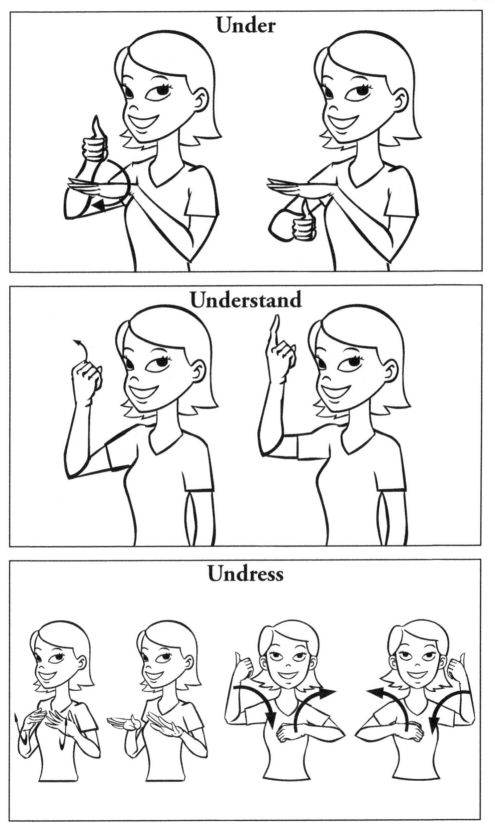

Under

Understand

Undress

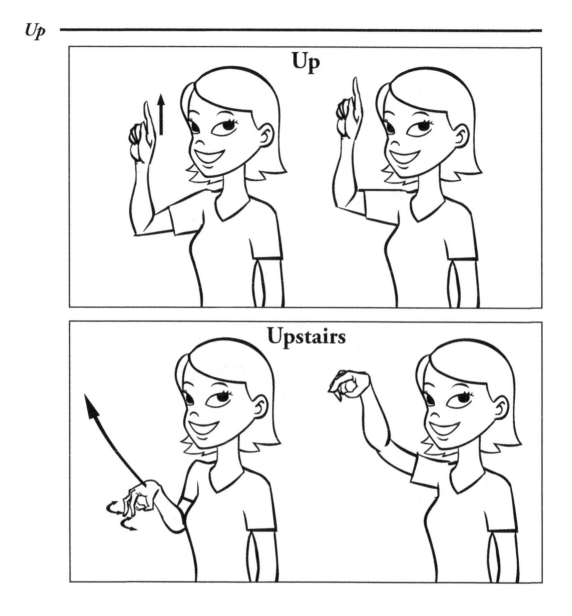

Up

Upstairs

Vv

v

Vegetable

Ww

Wagon

Wait

Wake Up

Walk

Wall

Want

Warm

Wash

Wash Hands

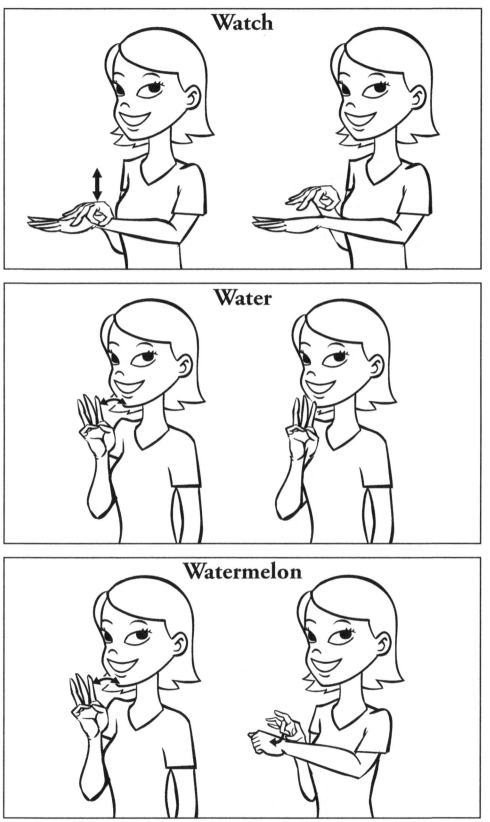

Watch

Water

Watermelon

Wear

Wedding

Welcome

Wet

Whale

What

Wheel

Wheelchair

When

Who

Why

Wind

Window

Wolf

Woman

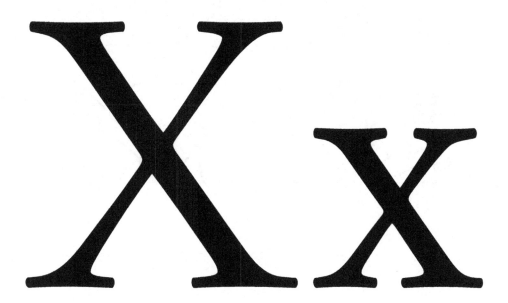

X

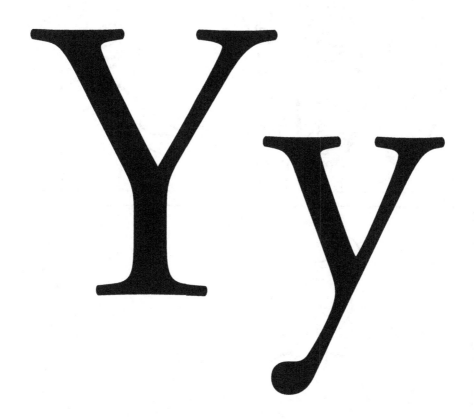

Y

Yell

Yellow

Yes

Yogurt

You're Welcome

Yucky

Zz

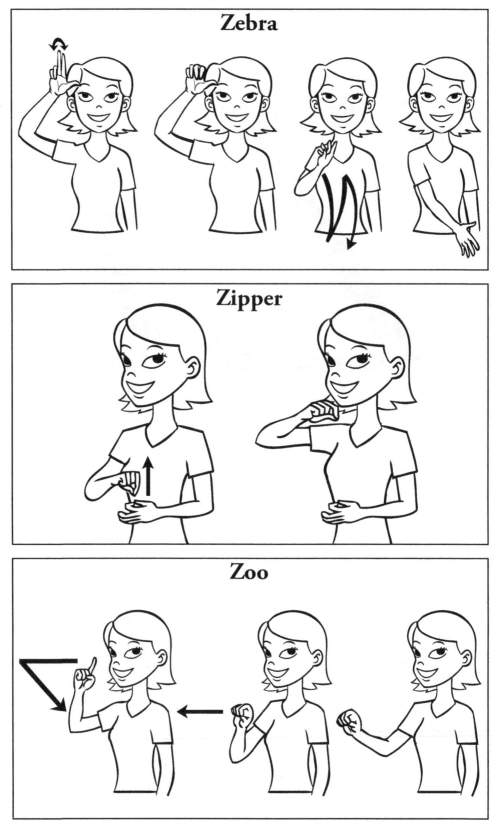

Zebra

Zipper

Zoo

Numbers

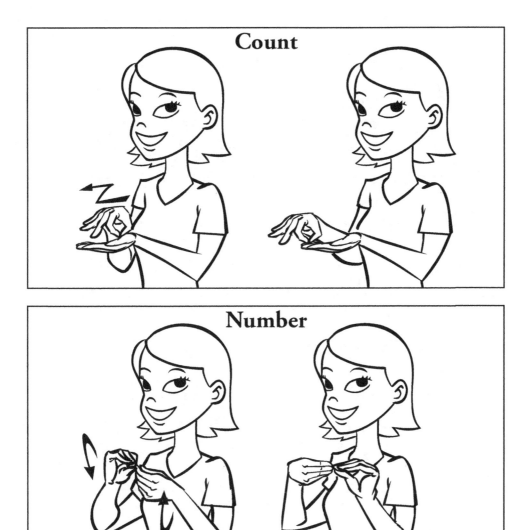

Count

Number